Virtual Assistant
Startup Kit
What You Must Know

Paul Hafalla

Copyright and Legal Notice

Table of Contents

Dedication

To my loyal hyperactive miniature dachshund pet 'Boo' who continuously gives me unconditional love and teaches me how to be patient, caring, loving and kind.

Introduction

In the online world, there are thousands of jobs being offered. One of those is that of virtual assistant. This can be a lucrative business online, and thousands of people have achieved success with this kind of career.

Now, if you are someone who wants to take control of your time and work within the premises of your home as a virtual assistant, you need to know the basics. As a newbie, you may earn a decent amount, but as you progress on this kind of job you can surely earn more and turn it into a full time job. So here is the introduction to the beginners guide to becoming a virtual assistant.

Create Your Own Workplace

Creating your own workplace at home entails having a designated work area that's quiet and gives you the flexibility to implement your virtual assistant tasks. Also, you need to have your own computer, a strong internet connection and other necessary virtual assistant equipment such as phone and fax machine, as well as pen and paper for your offline tasks.

Make sure that your computer has an advanced processor, added memory and a hard drive. This way, you can download, upload and install the programs needed for your everyday work as a virtual assistant. Of course you need a mouse, keyboard, computer headset and web cam.

Your internet connection should also be fast enough to easily download and upload programs to your computer. This will allow you to communicate with your client without any hassles at all.

Present a Captivating Resume

Now, after making your own work area, you can create your resume to present to clients willing to hire you. Note that your resume should have information regarding your skills, qualifications and work experience.

The point here is that you need to provide necessary information in your resume, which will ensure that clients are interested in hiring you to be part of their online company. However, be honest, since displaying honesty is a part of being a virtual assistant.

Use Online Tools for Your Virtual Assistant Tasks

Of course, you need to have the best online tools needed for your virtual assistant endeavors to make tasks easier. You can install such tools online, or your future client may provide you with them.

Negotiate Your Charge Rate

Applicable charge rates for a virtual assistant depend on the rate of your client. You may also demand a rate but if you are still a newbie, you might as well be contented with a flat rate. After you've had years of experience and acquired advanced skill as a virtual assistant, you may stipulate for an increased rate. But even then, negotiating your rate with your client is the best thing to do.

Harness Your Virtual Assistant Skills

Since you are just a beginner virtual assistant, you may need to harness your skills by learning online. There are lots of resources detailing how to gain skills in article writing, transcription or data entry and more. Be patient, and in time, you will definitely understand the basics as well as the advanced tasks required of a virtual assistant.

So, if you want to be a virtual assistant and earn more money than you usually do, then be patient, create a compelling resume, learn the skills of a virtual assistant and even use online tools to make tasks easier. In this way, you can become qualified as one of the best virtual assistants online.

Chapter 1

Common Work Space

Working at home as a virtual assistant is very beneficial, both, for employees and employers, for the both parties are able to easily cooperate online and get all the tasks ready and done as if they are working at the same office. The only thing you basically need in order to become a virtual assistant is a set of required skills and traits that make you feel competent in that profession, along with solid internet connection and PC.

On the other hand, it can be hard for virtual clients to hire a virtual assistant who is the right fit for the job, along with finding the person who is competitive and has certain skills, which would qualify them for the job. Some of the most wanted traits employers are looking to find at their assistants are:

Availability – online business owner would want their virtual assistants to be available at all times. This also means that assistants should always be on the right schedule whenever they are needed. Take into account, virtual assistants should understand the needs of their clients, one of which is punctuality at work, even if it's only virtual task. "Virtual" doesn't mean that the job and time availability are less important. On contraire: this is the one thing that is maybe wanted the most.

Work-friendly Space – A virtual assistant should have a proper work area even if he or she is just working within the premises of their own home. Make sure that you can select one area in your home where you can find your peace and quiet. Also, you should have the right offline equipment such as your computer, table fax machine and other office supplies. By establishing work-friendly environment, you are ensured that you will be more productive, efficient and relaxed.

Honesty – Take into account that you are entrusted with your client's company, and thus you are considered to be a part of it. Basically, what your job comes to is handling very important information, of which many are of sensitive and classified nature (e.g. financial data, passwords and other important documents), which make you a steering wheel of the company you are working for. Make sure that you are always honest and loyal with your clients, contributing to great working relationship and long-term position with place for progress and development.

Responsibilities at Work – Remember, you are given the responsibility in making your client's job much easier, thus you need to be responsible and show what you are made of. There is no room for excuses or procrastinating. Your client is counting on you at all times, and in accordance with what is expected from you as from virtual assistant, responsibility is what simply has to be prioritized. If you are taking care that you are acting responsibly, you will surely be rewarded.

Besides all these aspects, where being a virtual assistant and helping your homeland by decreasing the rate of unemployment by being an employee at online companies, will also help you develop and grow professionally - there are also some other benefits in becoming a virtual assistant. Number one reason is that you will surely earn more: The fact here is that virtual assistants are paid in dollars and this could be on hourly, weekly, bi-monthly or monthly basis. Average virtual assistants rate would range from $5 and above and it can be per hour rates, which depends on the client, also being set in accordance with your skills and experience as a virtual assistant.

Another benefit is that virtual assistant can also be given bonuses. Remember, bonuses are given by clients if they are certain that you are a competitive and productive virtual employee, as shown in your personal performance. As a matter of fact, there are even some online virtual assistants who are given travel holiday bonuses along with pocket money, while some of them are given cash bonuses.

Judging by the numbers and statistics, being a virtual assistant can be more than rewarding. If it is your call to be a virtual assistant, you can surely choose this profession to be your career path. You can start earning well and you can even learn to operate and apply some online tools that are more than useful for your online virtual assistant endeavors.

Chapter 2

Internet Connection

When it comes to their daily work endeavors, internet connection is of immense importance to virtual assistants. Of course, you wouldn't even be able to read this eBook now, if you didn't have an internet connection.

However, it is not enough for virtual assistants to have only a simple, fast internet connection. A working virtual assistant must possess both a reliable and fast connection. That shouldn't be a problem as most IPS's (or internet service providers) today can offer you satisfactory services and make sure that your work schedule as a virtual assistant is always on the right track and that you are always able to meet your deadlines.

Keep in mind that internet service is quite affordable nowadays, so if you are working as a virtual assistant you will have no problem finding a cheap internet connection suitable for taking on your daily virtual tasks.

On the other hand, you might also need specific connection requirements for faster work transaction to some of your clients. That being said, connection speed may vary depending on where you live. For instance, here are average speed values of internet connection in some countries around the world.

India – 5.1 Mbps
USA – 24.4 Mbps

Japan – 29.0 Mbps
Philippines – 3.5 Mbps

Canada – 22.6 Mbps
Nigeria – 4.6 Mbps
Sweden – 48.1 Mbps

Pakistan – 2.8 Mbps

Remember, these are just some of the speed values provided by ISP's in certain countries. These also differ from the ping values of various internet providers, which is also important for quick, live communication. A ping of less than 100 milliseconds is already considered fast in some parts of the world. So, you can conclude that speed values vary from one country to another. Whatever the speed is, reliability of your connection is just as important as it ensures uninterrupted work.

You should take your time when choosing the right provider as some can offer better service than others, and at a lower price. That is why when you're first starting your career as a virtual assistant you must make sure that your chosen provider is capable of giving you the best service possible.

However, the quality of your connection will also depend on the plan you have applied for. For example, if you've chosen a flat rate plan your internet speed will be much slower, which can lead to problems. It is probably a good idea to choose a faster and more reliable connection immediately so that your career as a virtual assistant can blast off.

Now, in order to know exactly what the download and upload speed of your connection is, you can check out some of these free testing websites.

TestMy.net

Speedtest.net
InternetFrog.com

These websites will offer you an overview of your connection speed.

Of course, it goes without saying that a great speed and reliability of your internet connection mean nothing without a computer or a laptop that is able to support it. Always make sure that your computer is performing well before selecting your preferred connection.

Chapter 3

Resume

If you are applying on job web sites for virtual assistant work, you will need to build your own resume. Your resume is important since it is the document wherein clients are able to assess your skills and objectives for work. Creating a captivating resume is necessary to be considered for employment.

First, research web sites where sample cover letters and resume templates are provided. Simply input the keyword "sample cover letter and resume templates" into a search engine. Take time to view various styles and types of resumes and cover letters which are most appropriate for applying for virtual assistant work.

The following are important pointers on how to create a captivating resume and cover letter. Be careful not to use too many adjectives or be overly wordy. Stick with the facts. Simply state your strengths, accomplishments and skills which will be of value to potential employers.

Be sure to format of your resume correctly. While researching sample templates, you will see that there are various choices in aligning your document's structure. Read up on which formats are most applicable for people seeking virtual assistant work or the one that you feel is most suitable.

The first line on your resume should contain your contact information; name, home address, phone numbers and email address. Below your contact information or on your cover letter you need to include your job objective. Your job objective needs to be concise as this is where you will convey your work qualifications for the positions you are applying for. Pay attention to examples of strong objective statements while doing your initial research online.

Next, include all of your job qualifications. For example; when applying for a virtual assistant job be sure to incorporate all of your relevant work experience.

Some accomplishments may include:

- Proficiency in specific computer programs or software which pertains to online tasks required for virtual assistant jobs. Superior professional communication, interpersonal and language skills.
- Expertise and skill set necessary for virtual assistant jobs as required by the employer.
- Mastery in completing assignments within an employer's scheduled deadlines.

Include years and time frames of your work experiences in all prior virtual assistant jobs. Additionally, list your accomplishments for each job specifically. This is where potential employers will evaluate your capabilities when it comes to virtual assistant assignments required to be completed by you proficiently.

In the next section include your educational background. Although it is not necessary for a virtual assistant to have earned a diploma from a four year college, it is best to include relevant coursework and the time frame and location in which you completed it.

Include all certifications and awards you have earned. Add any virtual assistance conferences, seminars or groups you have attended or belong to. These will enhance your chances of being hired.

You may also convert your draft resume to PDF format for a more professional presentation. You may choose to a clear, recent and professional looking picture of yourself. You may also save your cover letter in a separate file so you can personalize it for each particular online company you apply to. Once you have created a resume to the best of your ability, it is time to post it to online job sites.

The next part of your virtual assistant endeavor is to research for additional technology regarding virtual assistant tools such as software and other programs. There are new applications constantly being created to better organize and make your work virtual assistant assignments easier. By learning to use new programs and keeping your resume updated, you will be better able to complete virtual assistant tasks successfully and become more marketable to possible clients, companies and employers online.

Chapter 4

Qualifications

Got what it takes to become a virtual assistant?

Virtual assistants are quite in demand currently and the need for this kind of workforce online has proven to be beneficial for both small and big businesses. Owners of businesses tend to hire virtual assistants off-shore because they offer cheaper rates but with high quality work output. Furthermore, virtual assistants would gladly "take a slice" of your workload, thus making your online business more productive with less effort and stress. They can also impart a good working relationship with you as their client and in turn provide a more positive online business outlook that would succeed.

There are tips to be considered for one to become a productive and competitive virtual assistant online. These include:

Proficiency in English – It is crucial for a virtual assistant to be proficient in English because English is the universal language which is widely used as a form of communication especially in the digital world.

Knowledge in using Online Tools – A virtual assistant should have the basic knowledge with regards to online application tools like Skype, Dropbox, Google Adwords, Google Docs and even in using email services.

Work Efficiency – Efficiency at work is a requirement for any virtual assistant to carry out activities skillfully. Efficiency means managing time and organizing every virtual task demanded by the client.

Dedication at work – This is also very important in ensuring there is increased result productivity at work.

What are the benefits of being a virtual assistant?

Working from home – As a virtual assistant, your home is your own office where you can work on your own pace and freedom which is convenient for a faster work output.

Less stress – There is minimum stress associated with being a virtual assistant since you can work in a nice and quiet environment (within your own premises) where you can even do some other tasks after finishing your online job.

Long-term Job – Working as a virtual assistant online offers job security. Some clients online may have many tasks at hand with limited time and with your help as a virtual assistant, you can have more work to do every time over a long period. However, it requires hard-work to meet the demands of the client

in due time to sustain a longer working relationship with potential clients online.

All these benefits and factors are essential in becoming an excellent virtual assistant. Therefore, learning the basics and even the advanced skills prepares the right work attitude of ensuring one is well prepared and compensated as a virtual assistant online.

Chapter 5

Services

There are so many services you could offer to provide to potential clients. Some of these require skills you may already have while others may require skills you may still need to master. Remember, the more virtual assistant skills you have, the more you can earn. This is a great deal for you. So when it comes to determining the services you can offer consider your skills carefully and consider how you can enhance your virtual assistant skills. Some of the services you can consider providing as a virtual assistant are:

Data Entry Service – This involves inputting computerized data in text or in numerical form in any a database or a spreadsheet using your computer keyboard. Data entry also includes audio transcription wherein you have to type an audio conversation file into a text file. The trick here is to have an attentive ear and to listen to the audio conversation carefully. Also be careful when it comes to your punctuation, spelling and grammar since this is needed to accurately type the conversation on the audio file.

Content Writing – Content writing involves writing articles in various formats to be posted on your client's website. Such articles can be keyword enabled (with or without links) or they can be simple articles that include rich content or information about your client's niche. They can also be press releases or newsletters. Remember that these articles are quite important for many clients since this is one way they can promote their websites and boost sales.

Online Customer Service – Being an online customer representative involves managing emails, online chat support and other online customer service tasks as requested by your virtual client.

Online Researcher – You can also offer to undertake online research services for your future client. This involves searching for various resources and information needed for the expansion of your client's online business. Provide the most accurate, most relevant information and remodel it into a feasible idea on how to market your client's business endeavors.

Social Media Manager – You can also manage the social media account of your client to boost their online presence particularly over social media networks. You should have the "charisma" necessary to attract traffic by posting relevant quotes, inspirational images and interesting comments or news to help promote your client's business.

Undertaking such service offers as a virtual assistant to your clients will surely help you reach online success. Remember, your job is to make your client's job online easier and successful.

Chapter 6

Tools and Software

Virtual assistants are skilled when it comes to any online tasks and some of the tasks they do on a daily basis are as follows:

Transcription Data entry Writing Customer support

Program installers (e.g. hardware and software installers)

Now bear in mind, all these tasks may not be done efficiently and on time without the aid of some online or offline tools which virtual assistants use. These tools, programs and other virtual assistant equipment are important to manage their job in an organized manner. So if you are vying to be a virtual assistant and make this as your full-time or part-time career, then you also need to have the necessary equipment to be used in your virtual assistant endeavors.

To make it easier for you, here are the needed tools and programs to become an efficient and organized virtual assistant.

A computer and Strong Internet Connection: For obvious reasons, you need to have a computer or laptop and a strong internet connection. It is best to have a computer that has the latest processor and operating system to install updated programs for your virtual assistant needs. Of course, a strong internet connection is very important. You need to inquire over at internet service providers (ISP's) and apply for a fast and reliable internet connection.

Email Address and Other Online Communication Services: You need to have your own email account. If possible you need to have more than one since you will need it in the event that your other account has crashed. Also, this is where you can communicate with your virtual client and complete work transactions. Other communication services such as Skype, Google Chat, WhatsApp, Google Plus Hangouts and Yahoo Messenger are also necessary if you and your client need to do a video call or a simple chat.

Virtual Assistant Software: Besides the pre-installed Microsoft Office (Word, Excel, PowerPoint, OneNote, Outlook, Publisher) on your computer, there are lots of additional software that you will need to be installed on your computer as a virtual assistant. These may be useful to install to guide you to your work:

Worksnaps
Dropbox Google Drive Google Docs

Screen Shot Software (Screenshot Monitor) Transcribing Software (Express Scribe) Spinner Software (Chimp Rewriter)

Plugins
Google AdWords

EverNote

Obviously, there are more of these programs in which you may need. Just remember, such programs can also be provided by your online client. This means you don't need to purchase all the necessary online tools since your client may have it and all they need to do is to share it with you.

Other Offline Tools: Take into account; you also need some offline equipment for fast paced work as a virtual assistant. You may need:

- A mobile or landline phone Tablet

- Fax machine Scanner

- Paper, pen and pencil Headset with microphone

Considering all of these will make your job easier and faster as a virtual assistant in the online world. It would compensate you well since you have the proper tools to do complete a job well done.

Once you are done downloading, installing and using such programs and other online tools for your virtual assistant tasks, the next task you will face after being hired by a possible client online is to consider talking about your wage. This is important and you will eventually know this once you converse with your client and come up with a "win-win" solution regarding your charge rate.

Chapter 7

Online Sites

Are you on a job hunt as a virtual assistant, and want to earn more than you do as an office employee? If this is you, then you can search for websites that provide virtual assistant jobs. Here is some valuable information about some of the top rated sites where you can look for job opportunities as a freelance virtual assistant:

oDesk – When it comes to hunting for a virtual assistant job, oDesk is indeed a reliable site. It has already provided more than a million job offers that range from writing, data entry, transcription, and even graphics tasks.

Freelancer – This is another reputable website that provides different job opportunities to aspiring and expert virtual assistants. Their wide array of job offers includes article writing, copywriting, translation, and other virtual assistant jobs.

Craigslist – This site provides high salary opportunity for virtual assistants compared to other online job-hunting sites. Then again, their job offers are the same as other online sites for virtual assistants.

Elance – This job-hunting site is also one of the most trusted in the online world. They provide work tools with regards to work contractor management. This helps organize invoices and other payment transaction details.

LinkedIn – LinkedIn is indeed popular for professionals who are posting their offers for possible virtual assistant employment. The profile of each account user is provided with details according to their skills and other descriptions. With this, employers can easily look at possible employees as part of their hiring endeavors for virtual assistants.

Fiverr - Fiverr is one of the uprising freelancing websites to date. With their five-dollar seller startup, who would dare miss such affordable yet promising services to get the job done fast and with high quality?

Now these are simply some of the online sites where virtual assistants can look for possible clients with high compensation. Remember, as a virtual assistant, you should also be skilled in meeting the demands of the clients.

When bidding for a job, provide your job description and ensure that your skills are also included. You should create a compelling résumé since this is what attracts the attention of clients.

Clients should be interested with what you have to offer just by reading your résumé. There are sites to help you start one or build yours up. Simply search "how to write an excellent résumé" or "online résumé templates" to find ways on how to write one.

Chapter 8

Rates or Fees

The fact is that you can be well compensated if you are working as a virtual assistant. This can be the case for majority of individuals who work as a virtual assistant online. But then again, there are certain factors with regards to how much a virtual assistant is being paid and they are according to their skills and experience in the field of online work.

However, again, such skills will depend on the virtual assistant as the fact here is that you are paid according to your skills and experience. Although you can say that you demand your own rate, this can be fair especially if you are bidding over at online job sites and will not always be the case since clients will always look for virtual assistants that offer the lowest rate online.

On the other hand, clients may also increase your rate after you've proven that you are indeed a competitive virtual assistant and are able to meet their demands accordingly with high quality output. For instance, you've been given transcription tasks and you have done it in due time with perfect transcription. Since you've done it perfect, your rate may increase and this is a good deal for you.

Further, you can also be given payout bonuses. This can be given if you have done well in your tasks and your possible client is more than satisfied with what you have done for them.

Take that into account, you can rate or charge your future client a virtual assistant and by this, you will surely learn to be more that may provide you both with a "win-win" solution. This is competitive online indeed important since you want to be paid according to your skills, but at the same time, clients would also want to get the job done efficiently at the right rate.

Consequently, the charge rates will also be according to where you're located. This is the trend nowadays and it means that the competition, when it comes to landing a job as virtual assistant especially in countries like India, Philippines and in other locations where virtual assistants are in demand, the charge rate would "play" around 5 – 10 dollars per hour.

However, some clients would pay every 15 days on a flat rate. This could be fine as long as the pay is just fair enough according to your skills and also if your contract is short-term or on a long-term basis. Just remember, the point here is that you are still well compensated.

Overall, charging your client will depend on your virtual assistant skills and experience and the more skills and years of experience you have, the higher your rate. Besides the rate of your job, you also need to impart your skills as part of your services. Again, this is crucial to having a high salary rate. So when it comes to the necessary services as a virtual assistant, start learning different tasks.

Chapter 9

Decorum

As a virtual assistant, you will complete work, remotely, for your clients. Your clients may or may not require you to communicate with them via audio or video. Some of your clients may prefer to communicate with you through simple messenger services while others may prefer to hear or see you work. In any case you must always remember that you are providing professional services, and even if you are working from the comfort of your home, it is no excuse to provide sloppy work.

If the client requests to communicate with you through a video feed or video, remember to dress at least semi-formally to give a good impression of professionalism. Even if you're not asked to present yourself through video or any visual medium, it would be a good idea to put on shoes to get in the mood to work. This is a common psychological idea, since the human brain associates not putting on shoes with home and therefore relaxation and putting on shoes with work.

Another important part of skill is English proficiency. It is just as important speak and write English, proficiently, along with impeccable grammar and pronunciation. If you don't know how to use words properly and skillfully, you will seem stilted. This is especially bad if a client requests you to write or re-write articles, letters, or speeches. Most of the time, your clients will request written work, as the client will not make it a necessity for you to speak perfect English. So my advice would be to read well written English books. Having a real interest in books can improve your written English skills, or any language, than countless lessons in the same language. Of course, you must choose good books. I recommend anything written by J. K. Rowling, Neil Gaiman, and Terry Pratchett. They are fantasy authors, who have a great command of the modern English language, and they are accessible authors.

The last and most important detail is that you must be punctual and courteous. Nobody likes getting held up due to delays. If you cannot be punctual or courteous then, it will be very unlikely for you to find employment or remain employed as a virtual assistant. Therefore, I would advise you to, at the very least, be predictable. If you are going to submit things late, then submit things late, predictably, like being always one day late. If you are going to be rude, then always be rude giving the client the impression that you are simply unable to be courteous. However, this is a very dangerous path and I would advise that you stay clear of it.

Your personality and oral and written skills, as well as the manner and style in which you do so, are just as important as providing good service, which helps you get paid. Human beings are socially and emotionally creatures not primarily logical ones. The more you follow my guidelines, the more successful you will be as a virtual assistant.

Conclusion

The virtual assistant profession is a rewarding job. There is freedom to provide quality freelance work without an immediate supervisor. The benefits are flexible work schedules and earnings that are substantially more than traditional jobs.

Online employment can be daunting for virtual assistants that are new in the business. While the benefits are attractive, there is more to consider than having an established area of expertise, adequate virtual assistant equipment, and necessary software and online skills. Good communication is the key.

A virtual assistant must have impeccable communication skills. English proficiency is crucial as the virtual assistant is in constant contact with current and prospective clients. Communication can be through email or live chat, but there are instances when verbal communication is required such as live video and telephone.

In addition to excellent communication skills, it is important to be fluent in the various technical programs and terms pertinent to the virtual world and workplace. Clients frequently submit programs, software and other online tools that may be unfamiliar. Good virtual assistants can edit, add images or publish articles using various office software and online programs.

Acquiring basic skills, good communication skills, and fluency in office software is the first step in a virtual assistant's career. The next step is employment. There are many career options and online employment sites. A virtual job search can be extended world-wide with the right search tools.

Having the right work attitude as a virtual assistant is an important aspects in the industry. Time management, quality work ethic, and superb customer service will set virtual assistants apart from others.

Overall, great virtual assistants possess all of the qualities previously mentioned. Your job search can begin now as this eBook has provided all of the qualifications for your new career. It starts now. Good luck!

Questions

1. What kind of virtual partner would you say you are? How would you accommodate the important abilities and attributes that are required by the customer?

2. How quick is your web association? Given the charges for your web association, the pace, and the pay that you get from your customer, would you be able to sincerely say that it is worth the cost?

3. Construct a resume and afterward following 48 hours, imagine that you are the client looking over your resume. Why would it be a good idea for them to pick you? Are there any particular things in your resume, in the same way as presentation or uncommon capabilities that could be useful or unfavorable to your employment looking for?

4. What are your capabilities? In the event that you feel that you lack a few capabilities, don't hesitate to add to it. Programming can be adapted by one's self in a couple of months; English style can be adapted by perusing great writing?

5. What would you be able to provide for your customer? Consider everything that much of the times are helpful for a virtual associate. Envision that you have your partner to help you with what you will be asked to do, and ask yourself what you would make them accomplish for you?

6. What are the great programs to have on your computer to help with your work? Obviously this relies upon the things that you are consistently asked to do?

7. Where do you anticipate hunting down virtual assistant employments? What is your plan to hunt them down? What are the sorts of customers that you are searching for?

8. Given your aptitudes, capabilities, and the capacity to pay of your customer, what amount do you think you ought to charge them?

9. How must you act in your occupation once you have it?
10. Lastly, after perusing through this whole manual, would you be able to sincerely say that being a virtual collaborator is for you?

Example Forms

As a bonus, I made some key structures which you can uninhibitedly utilize. These structures are sample resume in text and PDF forms (this serves as an issue in making your resume in MS Word or Photoshop), presentation document, contract & assention, month to month income, work format, receipt and survey & appraisal. You should simply download all these structures here http://1drv.ms/1tusLph. When you finished this, you are obliged to alter it. Erase and supplant a couple of words in the body, header and footer of the structures. Likewise, supplant the specimen photograph or logo with your own.

Case Studies

Case Study #1
Do I Need to Present an Agreement?

The Case

My regular client from Australia proposed a job for me. It entails working as his regular online virtual assistant. The job will start off as a part-time position that will eventually become a full-time job. His proposed rate is awesome, which will be paid one month in advance, and includes a one-month bonus after 6 months if he's satisfied with my virtual assistant services. This job will commence on Dec 1st.

The Question

I considered presenting an agreement form. I asked myself, "Do I really need this form?" In my quest for answers, I started to search the web in order to get some ideas and insights on what to do and how to create a simple form. Some sources said it's important; others said its okay with or without an agreement form.

What Did I Do?

I decided to present an agreement form to this client. When I was done writing the form, I emailed my final draft. He read it, agreed, and signed. I felt satisfied, as he signed the contract and agreed to the terms. I wasn't expecting that this contract form would be so easy for both of us. Thankfully, it turned out to be alright.

Lessons Learned

I learned how to create a simple agreement form. I also learned about its importance. You can freely use and copy the agreement form that I used, here.

Case Study #2
How I Recreated My Image?

The Case
"You can't serve two masters at the same time."

This is absolutely correct. I am currently marketing myself and my abilities as a creative virtual assistant. Before I chose this, I created art as well as serving as a virtual assistant. Evidently, I have made the decision to hibernate my creative talent for an undetermined length of time. Now, to portraying my role as a successful virtual assistant. Why?

Two years successively my creative career online did not progress beyond any sales. In fact, it plateaued into the midst of melancholy, not making any sales. I have done all I have been able to portray my image as a visual artist online. This included networking with other artists, managing a hi-stat artistic blog, joining a range of art groups online and offline, and participating in a variation of gallery exhibitions worldwide, online, etc. This made me question why this had happened. My art is not in question because I could say it is at an acceptable standard and other critics appreciated it. I have had mentions of various art galleries and blogs online to multiple awards.

The Choice
It is a tough decision to make because I love doing both creative work and being a virtual assistant. But I feel I have to give up one and go on with the other. As a result, I chose the path of becoming a successful virtual assistant. Why? Honestly, I am a man with limited resources so I need a stable career to live on.

But, what is personal brand?

Basically, it is a strategy of marketing yourself as a brand- not literally selling yourself but your skills and talent within a field. This trading strategy is being practiced all over the world. Successful personal brands are actors/actresses, business owners, and many others. Example of which are Donald Trump, Justin Bieber, etc.

How I recreated my image?

When I made the decision to be a VA, I planned within a few weeks on what to do. First, I rebranded my website. By this I mean I have given up the old blog and now design and managing a personal VA website (paulhafalla.com) and even manage this blog. I also reshaped my networks into the right people who have the same interest, which is now virtual assistance and not art. I have already established successful freelance portfolios on Fiverr, oDesk, and Elance. So, I interconnected everything- even my social media.

The Result

Success! The choices I have made now define a brighter, promising future. All the hard work has paid off. I am already earning money. I have not reached the status I aspire for on my online career but I will get there soon. When I reached that level, it will be helpful not just to me but also for my loved ones.

Case Study #3
Should I Charge Clients Additional Fees?

What kind of fees?

I am pertaining to fees deducted by PayPal, wire transfer etc., before your money gets transferred to your bank account. I think that it is the thing they call "service fee". Before I get my hard-earned money as cold cash, it will take a rigorous process like this. I believe this doesn't happen to me alone, but also with other people around the globe who are using the same system as I do online on the web or as a regular business transaction.

How did I approach this case?

Honestly, I'm not charging any of my clients' additional fees when it comes to this matter. It is my way of thanking them for availing my services in return for doing a job for their business.

I was wondering if it is appropriate to charge clients additional fees for these kinds of services. I would like to ask your point of view and advice about this.

Case Study #4
Should I Spend Vacation With A Client?

The Proposal

A client asked, "Where are you from the Philippines?" "From the province of Pangasinan in Luzon," I replied. "My friend and I will be visiting Cebu in the Visayas region so this is our chance to meet and spend a 2-day vacation," client replied. "Cool," I replied. "But, I'm not sure if we should meet or not because I'm shy," I replied. "Don't worry, it will be all company's expenses," client replied. "When would that be," I asked. The client replied, "On March 2015." "Okay, but I'll think about it and message you before that time," I replied. "Okay," client replied.

Why I Didn't Say Yes?

I have my own discretion when it comes to meeting clients. First, I am really shy. I never experienced in the past spending a vacation with my client or boss from another country. Second, my emotions are mixed up on that day of our conversation via Skype. I felt excited at the same time worried then all of a sudden negative thoughts popped into my mind.

Consultation with Someone

Because of this mixed emotions, I tried to consult my friends and relatives on whether or not I should spend time with my foreign client. Most of them said "yes" explaining the benefits of leaving my hometown and spending time somewhere far away. Also, they say it will be beneficial for us to get to know your each other in hope for friendship, business or future career plans. In social media, like Spring.

Me they say "no." I asked them why. Some say their client or boss is horrible, a boss from hell. So, why should they spend time with their client? It's a recipe for disaster.

My Final Decision

The meet up or 2-day vacation will be on March 2015. I only have a few weeks left to decide. Honestly, I don't know what to do. I can't decide right now. I have fears and some negative thoughts about it, but hoping for a positive. Whatever I decide, let's just all hope that I won't regret it. That's my decision for the time being.

Case Study #5
Stretching My Arms

The Case

I'm surprised and overwhelmed with old, regular and new client virtual assistant gig offers that I receive on a weekly basis. They are numerous. These offers come from freelancing websites, direct emails or social media. Some of which are easy or not tasky but mostly time consuming. Honestly, I don't bother if they are time consuming as long as the client's proposed rate is good and I can attest to do the gig and deliver it on time with good quality. But, there are moments in time that I need to "decline" offers which makes me feel sad sometimes.

The Problem

Declining offers from client(s) due to lack of time. This is the main problem I'm encountering now. I have 2 regular clients. My job roles are online admin assistant and online virtual assistant. The schedules are 8 am till 1 pm for the VA role and 3 pm till midnight for the online admin assistant role. This is an ongoing basis, 5 working days schedule. Sometimes I do accept sideline VA offers from freelance websites. But when these sideline offers become numerous on a given specific week or day, I have no other choice than to decline the offer(s).

How Am I Planning to Resolve The Problem?

I tried to manage or stretch my time, but it has given me a lot of stress when I'm overloaded with sideline tasks to do on a daily basis. So, I have decided to "stretch my arms" for these types of offers. How? I have started to create a freelance group named Genesis

Team. This is a team of virtual assistants, which I'm planning to hire. They will be selected from freelancing sites. They will only help me on as needed basis whenever I'm overloaded with too many sideline tasks to do in a day or week. My role here becomes a team leader assisting VAs and checking or correcting their draft tasks and finalizing each before we send it to client(s). The rate that I'm planning to offer to my team is 50/50. The first half will be given to my team and the other half, which I'm planning to keep.

Conclusion

I hope this plan will work and hopefully I will not regret losing new tasks offered by various sideline clients.

Case Study #6
Unpaid Fixed Rate Service

Sad, worried, depressed, angry and miserable. These were my feelings when a client didn't pay for my services. Do you also feel the same way when someone makes you feel stupid? After you complete the task and submit it, all you get are ignored messages and no payment.

The Client & Task

I logged into a website one day to check for messages and recent job posts. The site, oDesk, is one of the leading freelancing websites. While browsing pages on this site, I came across a 'transcription' gig that was posted by an Australian client. His profile on oDesk seemed trustworthy. It had reviews and previous hires with the rates. So, I read the task and proposed my rate. He picked me out of all the 20 people who had posted their offers. . We later agreed on a specific rate and terms. One of which was to complete the work within 3 days, after which he would remit the payment. Eventually, I completed the task and sent the transcript in MS Word format. Of course, I submitted this document through oDesk.

I was aware of the fact that this was a FIXED RATE GIG. I also read the pros and cons of 'fixed rates' in oDesk. One of oDesk's policies is that they have no control over 'fixed rates'. This means that they cannot guarantee if a freelancer will receive payment or not.

How I Resolved This Problem

I decided to file a complaint with oDesk's Help & Support team. Why? I had already sent multiple messages to the client regarding the payment. To my dismay, I never received any response or payment. After a few days, I received a reply from oDesk's support team regarding the issue. Sadly, as I expected, they could not resolve the problem. I requested the support team to ban the client from oDesk which they categorically stated that they could not do so. They have no control over the clients!

The Outcome

I really regret why I chose to transcribe this client's audio transcript. I feel I wasted so much of my time and resources on the work. It was almost 98% accurate; it was a high-quality transcript. One of my regrets is that I trusted the client to an extent of not requesting for a down payment prior to working on his order. I should have at least required an initial payment. If I had proposed this request maybe the client would have been compelled to make the full payment.

I learned a lot from this ordeal. I have decided 'to be picky' from then henceforth. More specifically when it involves fixed rate jobs in oDesk or other freelancing websites. This is one of the major problems with freelancing websites. There's no guaranteed payment for fixed rate jobs. In some cases, even when the client makes the initial payment, there's still no guarantee that they will pay the remaining balance.

Regardless of the risks involved in online work, I do love transcribing. In fact, I just recently transcribed a video interview from a trustworthy client. I converted the MP4 video into MP3 format to easily transcribe it. Why? Because I'm using a transcription software that only requires MP3 format documents. My transcribing life is made easier with the use of this software. . Of course, this is a TRUSTWORTHY oDesk CLIENT. He completely sent the full payment for my services.

Case Study #7
When Your Services Are in Question

The Case

One day, while working late at night, a regular client called unexpectedly at 10:00 P.M. He is a businessman from the U.S. who I've been working with for many months now as a virtual assistant. From the tone of his Skype message, I could tell he was mad. Then, when he finally called, he said, "We're removing you from the team. This is your last day." My first reaction was a state of shock. Then came so many questions in my mind about what I could have done wrong.

The Problem

Plainly, there was a card issue. He said what he said because I had charged his client's credit card. I'm handling his business payment system; that's my primary role. I do some other extras in between, such as booking appointments, PhotoShop, etc. Since I'm well-versed in all facets of virtual assistance, we had agreed to this term – a multi-tasking job. The issue was he had viewed his calendar appointment, but he had never opened that particular client's calendar.

How I Resolved the Problem

My client missed reading the words "cancelled – to be charged" on the client's calendar. I politely said, "Sir, kindly open that client's calendar again on that particular time and day." And so he did. He read the exact phrase about which I'm speaking. "I'm sorry, Paul. You're right; this client's card should be charged," he said. "That's okay," I said. "We're not removing you from the group," he said. "Thank you," I said.

Conclusion and Advice

What a relief to hear that I still had my job. I'm glad my client came to realize his mistakes from this issue. I've been doing my best for his business as a V.A. from the very beginning. This is the first time my boss got pissed off because of a misunderstanding.

Dissecting the issue and giving solutions immediately will resolve potential problems. Controlling your emotions, being respectful and kind while resolving issues is vital to maintaining professionalism in your conversations with your boss. This is how I reacted to an unexpected situation. It's important to remember that we are all humans who are prone to make mistakes; our boss is no exception.

Case Study #8
Writing a Critical Press Release

Have you ever been approached by your client to write a press release? I mean not just an ordinary press release to promote a product, book or website. By writing a press release, there's a possibility that you'll get involved.

Honestly, I'm not a top caliber author, writer or journalist. I'm just an ordinary blogger with poor command of the English language. One day, the client accidentally browsed my 'old' hi-stat blog named 'Pa Ul' on the web. He got impressed with its simplicity and content. Because of this, he sent an email inquiry about writing a press release. Since I'm a freelance virtual assistant, I responded and accepted his terms and proposal.

The Client

The client is an American Catholic ordained priest. For privacy reasons, let's keep it by the name as Father Paul. The priest has been assigned somewhere in the Far East. He serves his priesthood for many decades at a local seminary there.

The Problem

Father Paul, the client, stated bit by bit his case via email. To support his concern, he sent some documents such as videos, photos and forms. According to Father Paul, the child was being abused by the mother so he intervened in the situation. For a few weeks, he took care of the boy. He provided him some shelter, food and clothing. Eventually, he felt a 'fatherly love' to the child. So, he decided to talk to the mother about his plans, he wanted to adopt the boy. At the tail end of their conversations, the mother eventually agreed.

One day, unexpectedly, the mother of the child reneged on their agreement. According to Father Paul, the mother made up some accusations about him. The way I understand the situation, he is being legally sued for pedophilia by the mother.

He wanted justice and was eager to prove his innocence. The case was under investigation by the local court at that time. In spite of this, he thought of sensationalizing his case through the media. He produced and published some videos and articles on the web. Now, he wants to have a press release in English and a local language. He's planning to send this to a local media publication.

How I Resolved This Problem

"I've written some press releases but not like this one," I said to Father Paul. I explained to the client, the priest, that this will be my first time to write something serious or critical. "If I accept his offer I will be involved," I said to myself. "I haven't decided about it yet. I'll let you know." These were my last messages at that time.

After 2 days, I messaged the client and decided to write the PR. Why? "Putting myself into your shoes made me decide that I should help. Though I haven't heard the other side of the story yet, but okay I'll do it," I said. I also said that, "I have faith and believe in your sincerity and honesty." I hope he understands what I mean by saying that.

Outcome

Father Paul and I agreed to some terms. In 2-3 days, I've sent the press releases both in English and a local language to him. I have second thoughts of sharing the PRs or not. But some of this blog readers and followers insisted. So, here are the PRs 'Young Boy Abused - Rabbi to the Rescue' and in Philippine Tagalog 'Bata Biktima Nang Pang-aabuso - Rabbi Sumaklolo.' He was impressed with the two written press releases. Eventually, he sent the PRs to a local media publication there.

The following month, the priest updated me on the issue. This time he requested of me to write an article. So, I've written the article 'Injustice for a Poor Priest' and send it to him. "This will be sent to a newspaper company," he said.

I'm in luck and still haven't heard of a court message yet till now. Since then I have no idea what happened to the case of Father Paul. Perhaps I'll follow up on this soon.

If you were in my situation, what will you do? Will you accept the offer of this client or not? Why?

Case Study #9
What I do when a client doesn't know what they need me to do?

Frankly, I've been in this circumstance a couple of times. The potential client assumes I'm a mind reader who can find out precisely how their business works, what they need doing and how I can assist them. I employed these strategies to bail potential clients work out what they require:

I asked them to write on a piece of paper with a pen every activity they manage over the course of the following week. Consequently, from that list, I hollered for them to check in red everything they need me to do as their virtual assistant such as task, writing, transcription, etc. Furthermore, from that list they will check it with a yellow highlighter all the tasks they will continue to manage and outsource to me every other activity not on their to-do list. They don't need to shade everything, apparently.

Or...

I demanded them to write down tasks that engage them longer than 30 minutes to execute. Therefore, highlight in yellow tasks they don't want to carry out themselves or don't care doing. Likewise, record work they need to execute, but not available for. I will advise them that they can outsource these tasks to form part of my business for the day.

In conclusion, after discussing these affairs with them, I'll eventually let them know the value and benefit they will get by giving me the opportunity of executing the tasks on their behalf. It will save them time, money and effort.

About the Author

Paul Hafalla is a seasoned home-based virtual assistant helping business owners and marketers throughout the globe in order to establish growth and development of their businesses. He lives in Urdaneta, Philippines with his mom, grandma and dog. This is his first eBook. Know more about Paul and the professional services he offers at www.paulhafalla.com

www.ingramcontent.com/pod-product-compliance
Lightning Source LLC
Chambersburg PA
CBHW071610170526
45166CB00003B/1042